For Daki, Mia and Matias without whom life would be meaningless…

Published by ExploreLight Publishing
Email: info@explorelight.com

First published: 2011
Printed in Ireland by Castle Print

Profile Pictures by David Earl
Design Ross Harrington

ISBN 978-0-9569108-0-6
© Peter Gordon

WILD GARDEN

Landscape Photography from County Wicklow
By Peter Gordon

Foreword by Éamon de Buitléar

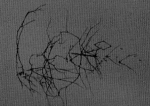

Acknowledgments

I would like to thank my family – Daki, Mia and Matias for the support and patience that has allowed me to put this project together. Landscape photographers do not keep regular hours and my passion is intimately intertwined with my work. Sometimes that can be difficult on the family dynamic so the most special thank you to the most special family.

I would also like to thank my parents first and foremost for bringing me into the world and taking care of me unconditionally through thick and thin.

My mammy always loved my pictures with absolute biased sincerity.

My father taught me nearly everything I know about making images and was the most important influence in the development of my photography, our business and this project.

A very special thanks to Éamon de Buitléar for writing the foreword. Éamon put some beautiful words together about the book that became the final piece in the puzzle in terms of the completion of Wild Garden.

I would also like to give special thanks to Dave and Daragh. Dave shot the biography pictures and has been immensely helpful in choosing which images to include and in the filming of the Wild Garden video. Daragh is a fellow nature photographer and has been hugely helpful in developing my own photography and in choosing what images to include within this book.

Thanks to the Gallery of Photography, especially Dan. They facilitated the scanning of all images. This was a key factor in the production of the book and exhibition and allowed the print process to do justice to the film.

Thanks to Ross Harrington for designing the book and bringing the professionalism and style that was needed to the layout.

Thanks also to Peter Farrell for making the Wild Garden video. He essentially directed and edited everything and without him it probably wouldn't have happened.

Thanks to Robert Towers. He was extremely helpful in the production and distribution of this book.

Last but not least thanks to Diarmo and JJ for reading through the text and making sure everything was shipshape.

I would also like to acknowledge and thank the following people and bodies for permission to use images captured on private land:

Garech Browne
Barbican International Corp. Ltd,
Luggala,
Roundwood,
Co Wicklow

Powerscourt Estate
Enniskerry,
Co. Wicklow

Select Vestry of St. John's
Cloughleagh,
Manor Kilbride,
Co. Wicklow

Foreword

By Éamon de Buitléar

Peter Gordon uses a camera but takes a painter's approach when he illustrates the hidden beauty that he discovers in the Wicklow landscape. His technique is to make full use of natural light in the countryside. Observing the conditions and patiently waiting for a change in the angle of light, Peter succeeds in capturing a rapidly changing effect. The moment captured seems likely to disappear in an instant, making the resulting images appear almost magical.

Choosing Wicklow, known as 'the Garden of Ireland', as a location was a wise choice; it has countless varieties of habitats stretching all the way from the edge of the sea up to the top of the longest continuous mountain range in the country. Wicklow is an inspiring location in which to work. Experimenting with tonal shades, composition and the climatic conditions on the day, a photograph, painting or piece of film can change forever a person's view of the landscape. I remember sheltering under a tree some years ago with a local man, while we waited for a shower to pass.

'Do you know' he said, as he looked out on the stretch of river winding its way down the valley below us.

'I never thought anything of this place and I've lived here all me life – no I never thought anything of it until a few years ago, when I saw a picture of it on a postcard down there in the little corner shop. There's no doubt but 'tis a lovely spot!'

Peter Gordon's skill is apparent in the pictorial results he has achieved where he is able to quickly catch the mood by making weather and light play their part. These images may make more people pause and look again at the scenery in other areas, which at first glance might have seemed quite ordinary. Early morning sunlight slanting across a mountain slope, a rising patch of mist in the corner of a lake, the reflected image of sky in a mountain stream or the snow laden branches of a tree at the edge of a wood; these are just a few examples of places where an opportune time of the day was chosen to give the desired effect to a particular scene. The images he captures during those fleeting moments are spectacular. Through his photographs Peter shows an awareness of what this environment has to offer, and his interpretation of the details in the subject, shows his personal connection to the surrounding landscape.

As I look at this collection of pictures I recognise
some of those woodlands, also the mountain
slope and the glacial lakes and I am reminded
of the many hours and even days, spent in those
same locations waiting for the sequence that I
hoped to capture on film for my documentaries.
Peter Gordon's wonderfully atmospheric scenes
show the beauty and richness of the Wicklow
landscape, capturing fleeting moments in time.
Browsing through the pages of this publication is
like a private view of the magic of the countryside,
which only some of us have the privilege of
witnessing in reality.

Éamon de Buitléar
Wildlife Documentary Filmmaker

Introduction

Wild Garden – Motivations

Five years ago I fell in love with the landscape of Wicklow. I was drawn to the rustic colour of its bog rivers, its rolling mountains and its colourful forests. Using traditional film cameras I wanted to put together a body of work that reflected the mood and inspiration I felt as I explored and photographed many corners of the 'Garden of Ireland'.

Beauty is of course subjective. 'Wild Garden' is a representative collection of images that I see as beautiful. They capture what I find inspiring and beautiful about the land. It is not by any means an exhaustive study of the county's makeup. The agricultural landscape and towns that embody large parts of the landmass have been deliberately omitted. I have ensured that every image within this body of work has been captured in Wicklow, however, 'Wild Garden' is not a documentary-style book. This geographical area has provided form and methodology to my desire to share moments of inspiration. I feel that despite living in Ireland, during this tough economic period, I can find some solace and continuity in the land.

As a child I remember walking on Kinsale Head. It was a typically Irish day with the wind howling and bands of light rain passed intermittently as the sky changed from grey, to dark grey, to grey. I will always remember the sense of awe when I saw those steep cliffs, that powerful breaking water, the deepness of the greens that hugged its edges and the darkness of the sky that lay overhead. It made me feel insignificant on one level but also deeply connected to my surroundings on another. As human beings I believe that we all have the ability to feel deep connections to our passions and experiences. As a landscape photographer and artist my passion is intertwined with the landscape, its intimate elements and the light that describes its beauty. This connection to the land, and the emotive feeling of just being present in something far more significant than oneself, is what has driven and inspired me to create 'Wild Garden'.

As I began to prepare this project my first port of call was to trawl through boxes and boxes of transparency film, or slides, to the layman. As I looked through each frame I was instantly brought back to the moment of capture. I could see more than just the shape of the land, the colour of its elements and the light that guided both my eyes and my senses. I could feel the emotion of the moment, the mood that defined my surroundings. The purpose of this project is to share more than light, shape and colour. The purpose of this work is to share with you the viewer the emotion that I felt at the point of capture, the mood that the land embodies and the beauty of Wicklow's landscape.

My eye and my heart have always been drawn to wild landscapes that feel untouched by man's presence. Exploring the Wicklow Mountains, as compared with a trip deep into the Himalayas, we do of course get a very different sense of scale. Nevertheless pockets exist in Wicklow, particularly in Wicklow National Park, where the land and nature feel unperturbed by anything that may concern human beings. The scale may not be on the level of places such as the Himalayas but there is a genuine sense of wilderness walking in the bog of the Sally Gap. Through this collection of images I have tried to share the inspiration I have felt while present in this wilderness. 'Wild Garden' has given structure and form to the emotive underpinnings of my creative leanings. My camera and Wicklow have provided me with an avenue to share what I feel when I see beauty in the land.

Beauty is subjective.

Wicklow's landscape is expansive, it is intimate, it is dramatic, it is moist, it is melancholic, it is inspiring and thoughtful.

Wicklow is beautiful…

Tight Grip

Close Embrace

Sprinkle of Magic

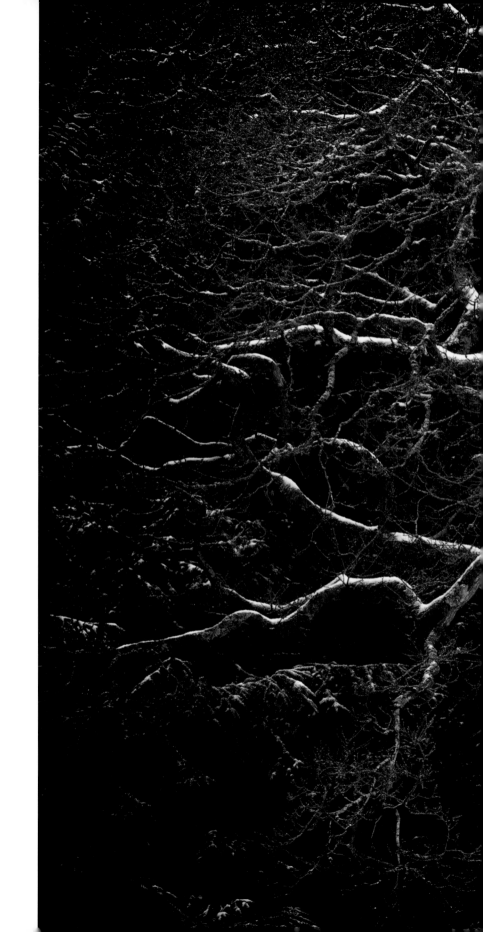

Organic Umbrella

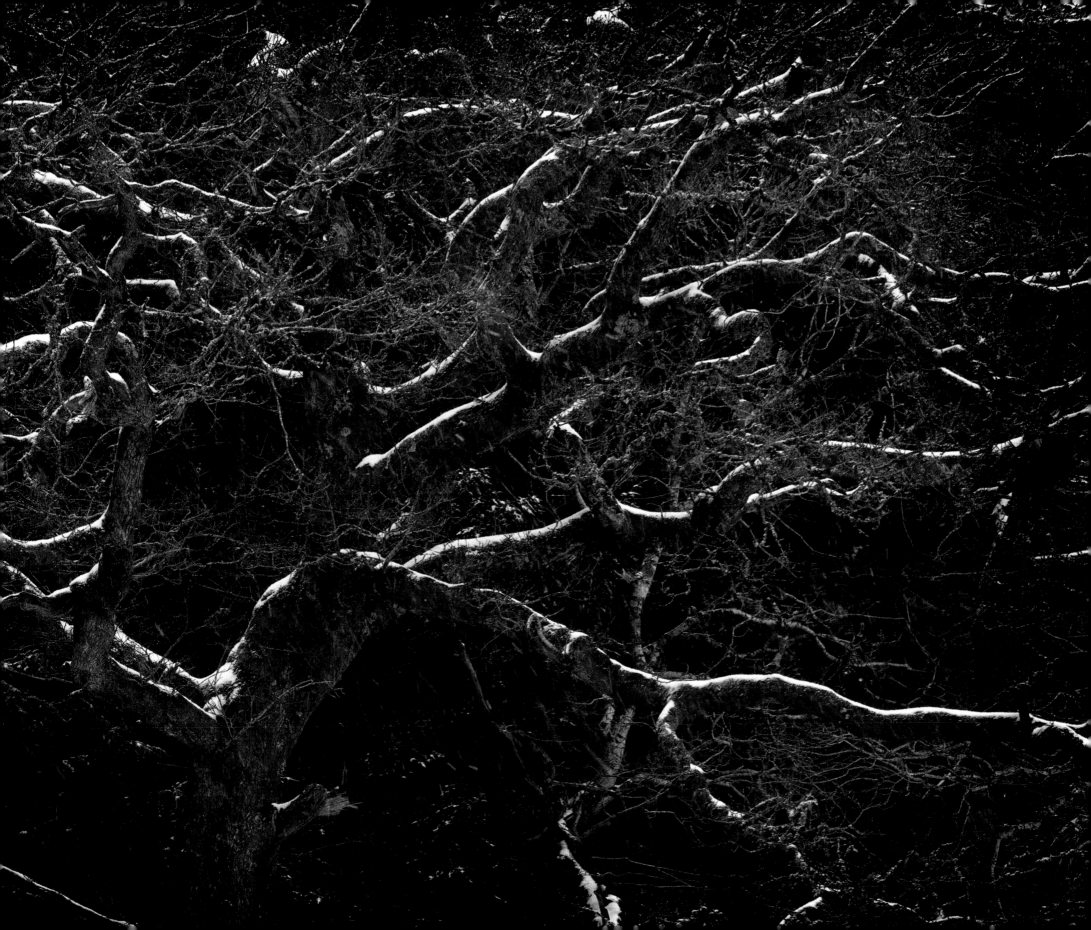

Outer Reach

Magic Dust

Snow Web   Raise the Curtains (opposite)

Arctic Lava

Winter Serpent

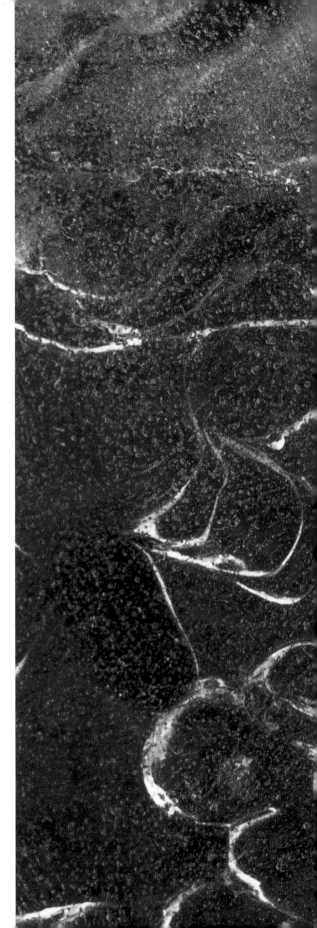

Nature's Rhythm

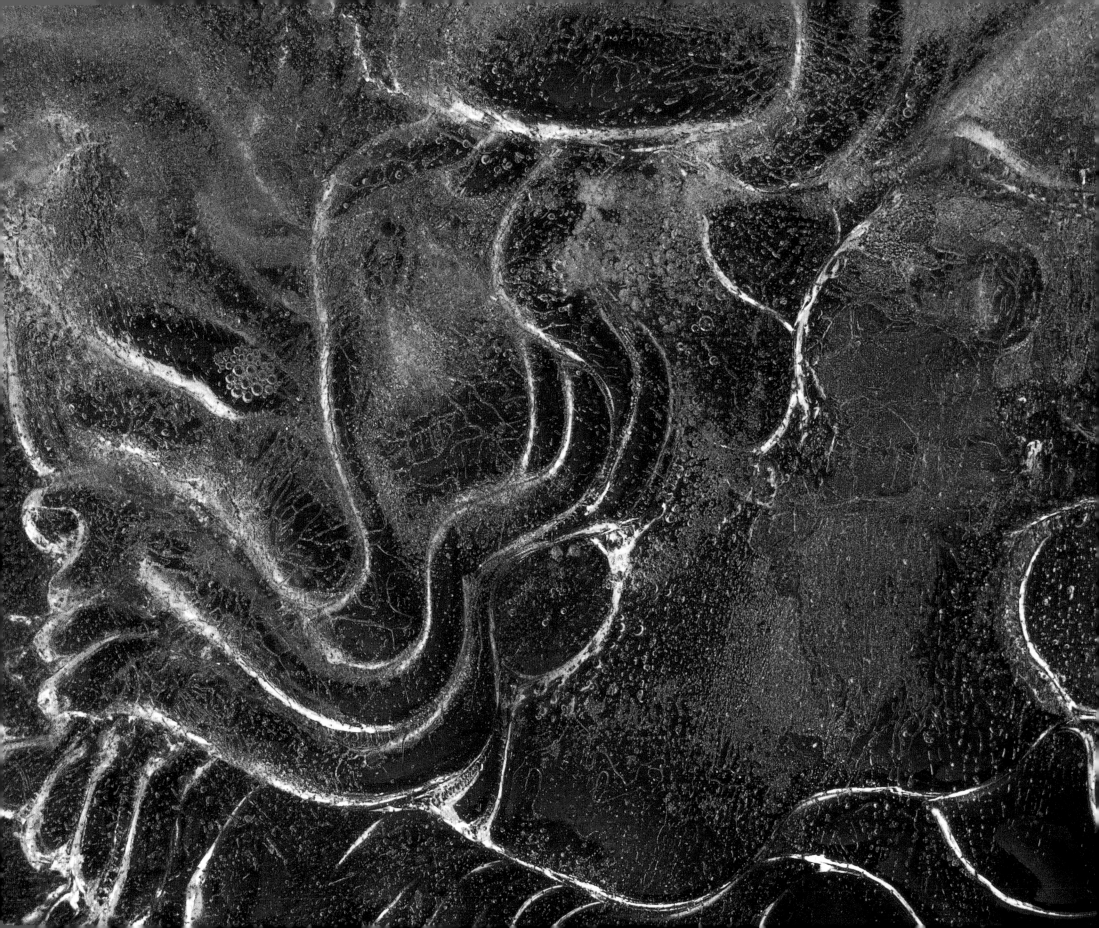

Organised Chaos

Elements' Edge

Winter Wonderland

Comfortable Isolation (opposite)

Pristine

Chilly Dip

Snow Swept

Snow Cavern

Voyage (opposite)

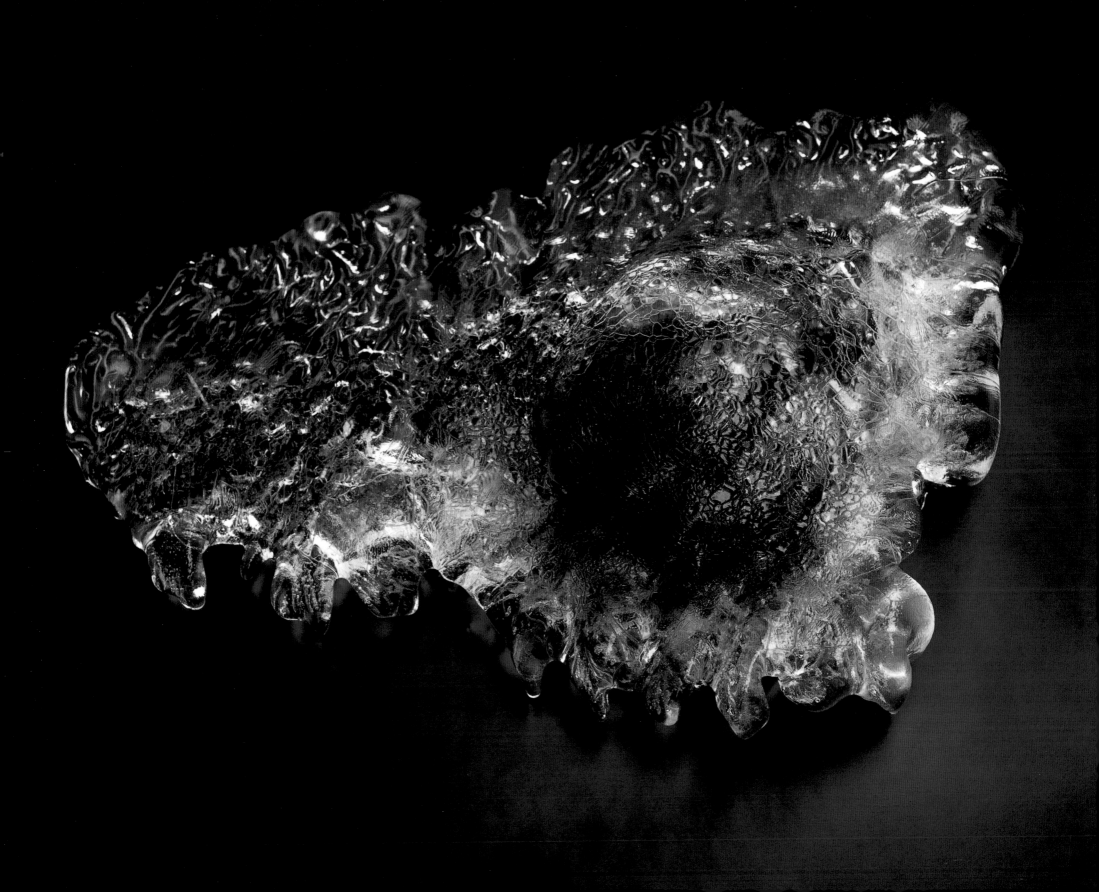

Frost Bite

Frozen Falls

Crocodile Scales

Winter Meets Spring

The Other Side

Savanna

Gentle End

Enthralled

Looking Up

Divinity

Emerald Rain Forest

Lush

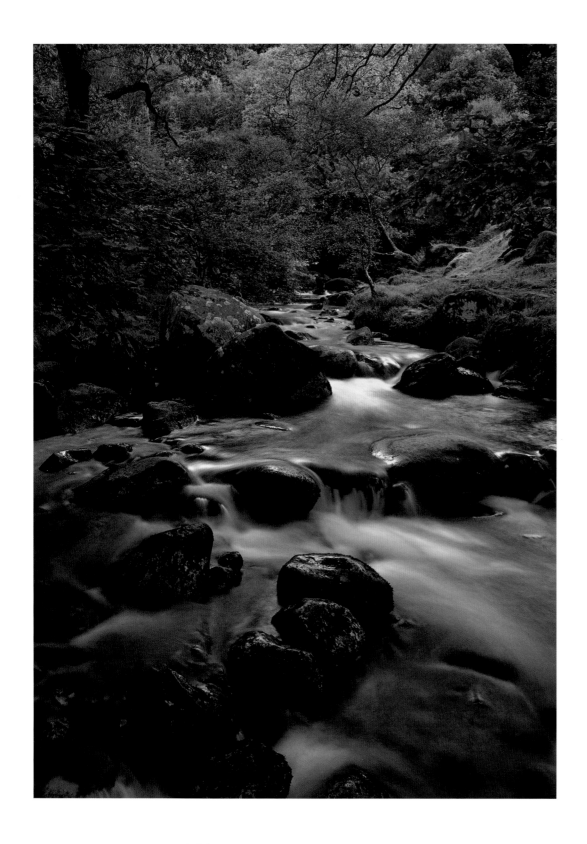

Golden Dawn

Meandering Growth

Line upon Line

Luminosity

Destiny's Edge

Dappled Touch

The Shire

Elder Statesman

Cool Dawn

Secret Depth

Rejuvenation

Onlookers

Swept Away

Standing Tall

Lines of Time

Purple Haze

Starry Eyed

Leading Lines

Breaking Storm	Nature's Blanket (opposite)

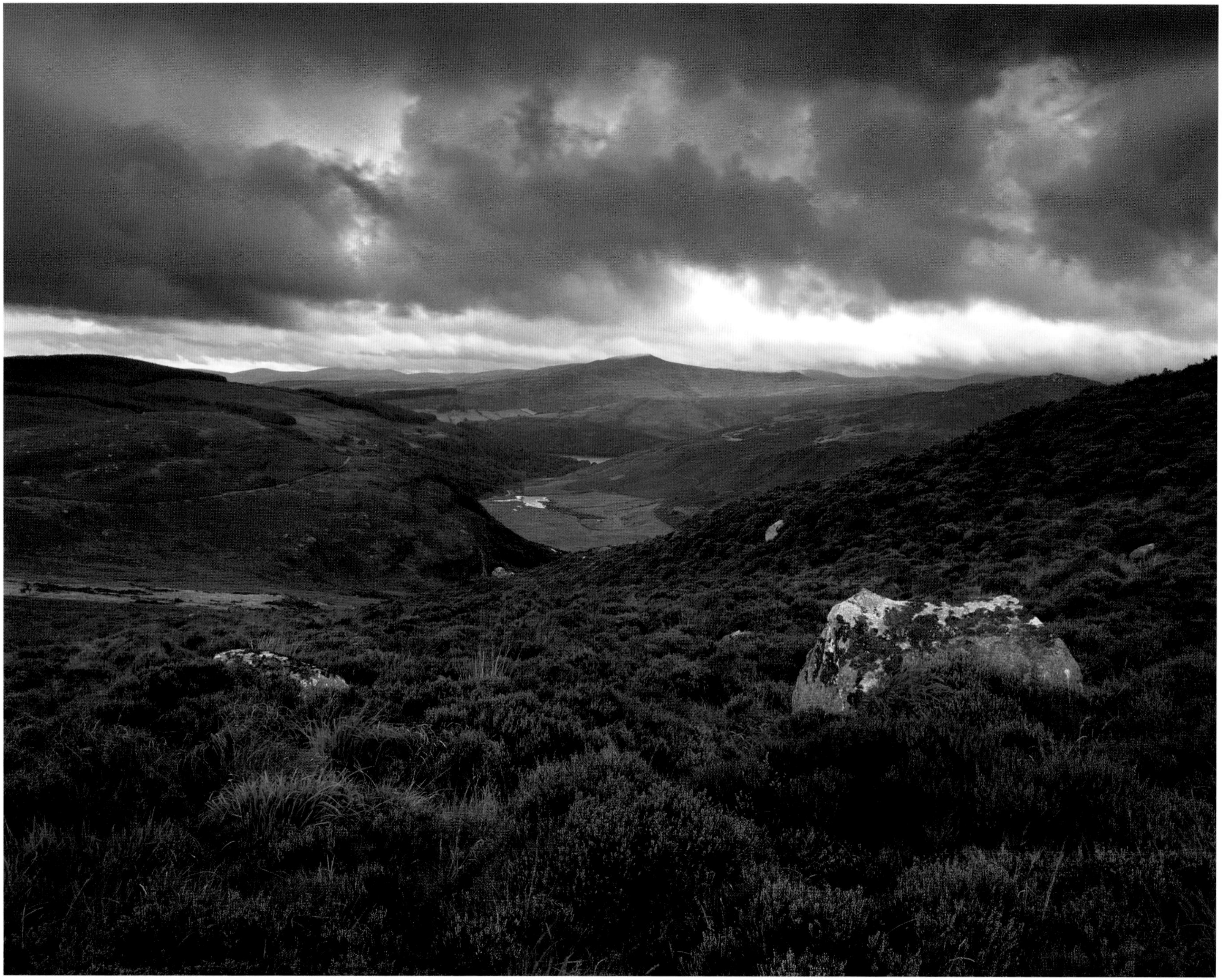

Stormy End

Waiting For The Day

Last Light Reflections

Moments Before Lights Out

Gale Force (opposite)   Peas in a Pod

Passageway

Wild Monument

Gentle Embrace

Going it Alone

Oriented (opposite)   Rising Above

On a Boat on a River

Animated

Silent Dawn (opposite)   Full Swing

Blanket Cover

Dead Calm (opposite)

Best Friends

Veins of Life

Burning Brightly

Crossing

Awakening

Still Dawn

Living Things

Amongst Living Things (opposite)

Gentle Sleep

Gold Rush

Amalgamation   Icon (opposite)

Tight Grip – Inchavore River

10

Close Embrace – Glenmacnass Valley

11

Sprinkle of Magic – Wicklow Gap

12

Dark Depths – Cloghoge River Tributary

13

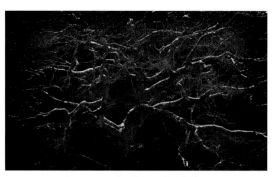

Organic Umbrella – Vale of Clara

14

Outer Reach – Ballinastoe Woods

16

Magic Dust – Wicklow Gap

17

Snow Web – Ballinastoe Woods

18

Raise the Curtains – Ballinastoe Woods

19

Arctic Lava – Cloghoge River

20

Winter Serpent – Inchavore River

21

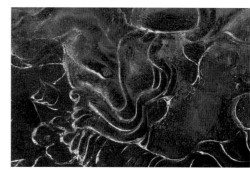

Nature's Rhythm – Cloghoge Tributary

22

Organised Chaos – Blessington

24

Elements Edge – Glendalough Upper Lake

25

Winter Wonderland – Distant Lough Dan

26

Comfortable Isolation – Wicklow Gap

27

Distant Observers – Vale of Clara

28

Pristine – Vale of Clara

29

Chilly Dip – Poulanass

30

Snow Swept – Sally Gap

31

Snow Cavern – Ballinastoe Woods

32

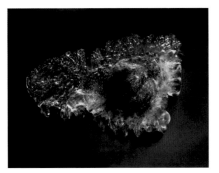

Voyage – Inchavore River

33

Frost Bite – Sally Gap

34

Frozen Falls – Inchavore River

35

Crocodile Scales – Wicklow Mountains

36

Winter Meets Spring – Wicklow Mountains

37

The Other Side – Wicklow Mountains

38

Savanna – Coronation Plantation

39

Gentle End – Source of the River Liffey

40

Enthralled – Lower Lake Glendalough

41

Looking Up – Powerscourt

42

Divinity – Vale of Clara

43

Emerald Rain Forest – Ow River

44

Lush – Ow River

45

Golden Dawn – Poulanass, Glendalough National Park

46

Meandering Growth – Glendalough National Park

47

Line Upon Line – Powerscourt

48

Luminosity – Hugging the Ow River

50

Wetlands – Cloghleagh

51

Destiny's Edge – Banks of Lough Tay

52

Dappled Touch – Knocknacloghoge

53

The Shire – Cloghleagh

54

Elder Statesman – Vale of Avoca

56

Cool Dawn – Lower Lake Glendalough

57

Secret Depth – Cloghoge Tributary

58

Rejuvenation – Cloghleagh

59

Onlookers – Wicklow Mountains

60

Dark Beauty – Powerscourt Waterfall

61

Swept Away – Inchavore River

62

Standing Tall – Coronation Plantation

63

Lines of Time – Coronation Plantation

64

Purple Haze – Lough Tay

65

Starry Eyed – Coronation Plantation

66

Leading Lines – Glenmacnass River

67

Breaking Storm – Glenmacnass River

68

Nature's Blanket – Glenmacnass River

69

Stormy End – Distant Lough Dan

70

Waiting for the Day – Glenmacnass River

71

Last Light Reflections – Inchavore River

72

Moments Before Lights Out – Lough Dan

73

Gale Force – Shot from Carrigvore, Wicklow National Park

74

Peas in a Pod – Coronation Plantation

75

Passageway – Cloghoge Tributary

76

Wild Monument – Sally Gap

77

Gentle Embrace – Cloghleagh

78

Going it Alone – Glendalough Lower Lake

79

Oriented – Glendalough National Park

80

Rising Above – Vartry River

81

On a Boat on a River – Upper Lake, Gledalough National Park

82

Animated – Glendalough National Park

83

Silent Dawn – Lower Lake, Glendalough National Park

84

Full Swing – Glendalough National Park

85

Blanket Cover – Devil's Glen

86

Dead Calm – Glendalough Upper Lake

87

Best Friends – Wicklow National Park

88

Veins of Life – Glendalough National Park

89

Burning Brightly – Vale of Avoca

90

Crossing – Scurlocks Brook

91

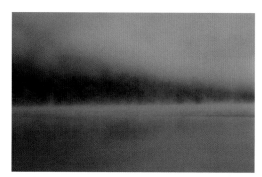

Awakening – Upper Lake, Glendalough National Park

92

Still Dawn – Lower Lake, Glendalough National Park

93

Living Things – Devil's Glen

94

Amongst Living Things – Devil's Glen

95

Moist – Cloghleagh

96

Gentle Sleep – Glendalough National Park

98

Gold Rush – Vale of Clara

99

Amalgamation – Cloghleagh

100

Icon – Upper Lake Glendalough

101

Technical details

Every image contained in this book has been captured on slide film. At the outset I was using a 35mm Nikon f5 (which I still love), but as the project began to develop I switched to a medium format Pentax 67 (which I still miss). Unfortunately my home was broken into in December, 2010 and the Pentax was stolen along with a range of lenses and other equipment. To complete the body of work I shot my final frames in April and May, 2011 on a Contax 645. All medium format lenses were prime and ranged from 55mm to 200mm. All equipment was loaded onto a Gitzo tripod with an Arca Swiss ballhead.

I have used a range of different Fuji films over the duration of the project depending on the result required. I favour Velvia 50 for intensity of colour and slow shutter speeds. However, it has the lowest dynamic range of Fuji transparency films so in situations of very high contrast I often switched to Provia 100. Provia produces colour more faithfully and has a greater propensity to hold detail in shadow areas. It lacks, however, the wow factor which has made Velvia the film of choice for many landscape photographers over the years. The final film I used was Fuji Astia. Astia has even less saturated colour than Provia but a greater dynamic range and is far less likely than any other slide film I have used to succumb to unpleasant colour casts and reciprocity failure.

After shooting the Wicklow snow for the first time on Velvia and Provia I moved to Astia as it provided me with the best means to produce the clean whiteness of the snow without loosing crucial detail in the highlights.

My circular polariser and my graduated neutral density filters were an integral part of my workflow. My polariser was used extensively to remove glare from running water and to slow down shutter speeds where necessary. I had (before the break in) a range of graduated neutral density filters ranging from two to five stops with different styles of graduation allowing me to keep skies in check and control dynamic range where necessary.